Who Was
Ronald Reagan?

Ronald Reagan ☆ 1911-2004

Who Was
Ronald Reagan?

By Joyce Milton

Illustrated by Elizabeth Wolf

Grosset & Dunlap • New York

To Rose and Mike—E.W.

Text copyright © 2005 by Joyce Milton. Illustrations copyright © 2005 by Elizabeth Wolf. Cover illustration copyright © 2005 by Nancy Harrison. All rights reserved. Published by Grosset & Dunlap, a division of Penguin Young Readers Group, 345 Hudson Street, New York, New York 10014. GROSSET & DUNLAP is a trademark of Penguin Group (USA) Inc. Printed in the U.S.A.

Library of Congress Cataloging-in-Publication Data

Milton, Joyce.
   Who was Ronald Reagan? / by Joyce Milton ; illustrated by Elizabeth Wolf.
      p. cm. — (Who was— ?)
   Includes bibliographical references.
   ISBN 978-0-448-43344-8 (pbk.) — ISBN 978-0-448-43345-4 (hardcover)
   1. Reagan, Ronald—Juvenile literature. 2. Presidents—United States—Biography—
Juvenile literature. I. Wolf, Elizabeth, 1954– II. Title. III. Series.
   E877.M55 2005
   973.927'092—dc22

2004020535

ISBN 978-0-448-43344-8   20 19

Contents

CONTENTS

Who Was
Ronald Reagan?

It was already dark, and the beach at Lowell Park was closed for the day. Dutch Reagan, the seventeen-year-old lifeguard, was helping the park manager, Mr. Graybill, close up the changing rooms when they heard muffled cries and splashing. A swimmer had sneaked into the park for an after-hours swim. Now he was in trouble, caught in the fast-flowing waters of the Rock River.

Dutch peeled off his glasses and dived into the dark water. He followed the sounds. A desperate man was struggling to keep his head above water. The swimmer was so panicky that he tried to fight off his rescuer.

Dutch was afraid the man would drown them both. At last, the swimmer was too exhausted to fight anymore. Dutch held the man's head out of the water and swam one-armed back to shore.

"PULLED FROM THE JAWS OF DEATH" screamed the headline in the Dixon, Illinois, *Evening Telegraph*. The paper called Dutch a hero, adding that he had saved twenty-five lives so far.

Dutch Reagan worked as a lifeguard for six summers. For the most part, the job was not glamorous. Early every morning, Dutch had to stock the snack bar. There was no refrigerator, just three big ice chests. So he would stop at the icehouse for a 300-pound slab of ice. After chopping the ice into three big chunks, he carried them, one by one, to the beach.

No matter how hot it got, Dutch didn't take a swim. The rule was that the lifeguard never got his suit wet unless he was in the water to save a life. The Rock River was famous for dangerous currents. In the past, people had been swept downstream. They had gotten trapped in the sluice gate of the dam. It had been up to the lifeguard to dive around the dam and get the body.

Dutch was proud of his work. Every time he pulled a swimmer from the river, he would carve a notch into an old log near his station.

After six summers, the log had seventy-seven notches cut into it. Patrolling the beach was hard work, twelve hours every day of the week, but Dutch enjoyed being responsible for the safety of the swimmers at Lowell Park.

Many years later, when he was known as Ronald Reagan, he became the fortieth

Ronald Reagan ☆ 1911-2004 ··

president of the United States. But Dutch always looked back on his days as a lifeguard as one of the best times of his life.

Chapter 1
A Boy Called "Dutch"

Ronald Wilson Reagan was born in Tampico, Illinois, on February 6, 1911. It was a snowy day, and his father left the general store where he worked and made his way home through the snowdrifts. Jack Reagan ran up the stairs to his family's apartment, a one-room flat on the second floor over a bakery. When he saw his new son, he laughed. "Why, he looks like a fat little Dutchman!"

The nickname stuck. The baby was known as "Dutch" all through his childhood.

Jack Reagan was a tall, handsome man who loved to tell stories and talk about politics. He was a good salesman. But every so often, he would go out and get drunk.

Ronnie

The Reagan Family

When Jack started to drink, he often ended up losing his job. Usually that meant that the family would have to start over in a new town. The Reagans moved a lot.

Although this often made things hard on Dutch, when he was older, Ronald Reagan remembered how much he appreciated growing up in a small town.

He said, "You get to know people as individuals . . . The dreams of people may differ, but everybody wants their dreams to come true . . . And America, above all places, gives us the freedom to do that."

Dutch and his older brother, Neil, were always the new boys in school. This didn't seem to bother Neil. He would find a group of boys to hang around with.

Dutch was more of a loner. He liked to hike along the banks of the Rock River, pretending to be a fur trapper of long ago. In one house the Reagans rented, Dutch found an old collection of butterflies and birds' eggs in the attic. He spent a lot of time studying them.

Dutch's mother was Nelle Wilson Reagan. Nelle Reagan was a very cheerful person. She always said that God had a plan for her life, so there was no reason to worry or feel sad.

Wherever the Reagans moved, Nelle always found some needy family to help.

She even visited prisoners in the jails, bringing them apples and crackers. Nelle never seemed to notice that the Reagans were poor themselves.

For Sunday dinner, Nelle would feed the family liver, not roast beef or chicken. Instead of hamburgers, she fried up patties made of oatmeal. They tasted awful!

Years went by before Dutch figured out that Nelle served these meals because she didn't have enough money to buy anything better. As a little boy, he thought his mother was just a bad cook.

When Dutch and Neil were little, Nelle read them stories every night. She would read

slowly and point to each word as she said it aloud. By the time he was five, Dutch was able to read the newspapers on his own.

Dutch read a lot of books, mainly boys' adventure stories. He read novels about Tarzan,

the king of the jungle, and novels about some characters called the Rover Boys.

Dutch also liked to draw funny pictures. He thought that when he grew up, he

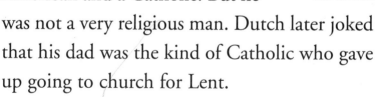

would like to be a cartoonist. Maybe he could draw his own comic strip.

Jack Reagan was an Irish American and a Catholic. But he was not a very religious man. Dutch later joked that his dad was the kind of Catholic who gave up going to church for Lent.

Neil usually followed what his dad did. So he became a Catholic, too. However, Dutch decided to join his mother's church. It was called the Disciples of Christ. He was baptized when he was eleven years old.

Nelle was against drinking alcohol. She even wrote a play about how drunkenness caused family fights. It was performed at her church. Although Jack Reagan promised to give up drinking, he kept going back to his old ways.

Even Prohibition, which made buying liquor illegal, didn't change him.

One day, when Dutch was eleven, he came home in the evening and found his father passed out in the snow, on the steps leading to the front door.

Dutch woke his dad up and helped him inside. He was angry and embarrassed. What if the neighbors had seen his father drunk?

When his mother came home, she sat Dutch down for a long talk. "Don't turn against your dad," she told him. "He has a sickness. He just can't help himself."

Dutch tried to follow his mother's advice. Anger was just a waste of energy. He would try to think positive thoughts.

PROHIBITION

DURING THE EARLY YEARS OF THE
TWENTIETH CENTURY, THERE WAS A
MOVEMENT TO BAN, OR PROHIBIT, THE
SALE OF BEER, WINE, AND WHISKEY.
WOMEN'S GROUPS CAMPAIGNED FOR
PROHIBITION ALONG WITH OTHER CAUSES,
SUCH AS VOTING RIGHTS, EQUAL RIGHTS,
AND EQUAL PAY.

A CONSTITUTIONAL AMENDMENT TO
PROHIBIT THE SALE OF ALCOHOL TOOK
EFFECT IN 1920. AMERICANS DID DRINK
MUCH LESS OVERALL. BUT PEOPLE WHO
WANTED TO BREAK THE LAW COULD FIND
WAYS TO GET AROUND IT. GANGSTERS

SMUGGLED IN LIQUOR FROM CANADA.
PEOPLE TRIED MAKING BEER AND WINE
AT HOME. ILLEGAL SALOONS, CALLED
SPEAKEASIES, OPENED IN THE BACK
ROOMS OF STORES, ON DARK COUNTRY
ROADS, AND IN OTHER OUT-OF-THE-WAY
PLACES. SOMEHOW THE OWNERS
MANAGED TO STAY ONE JUMP AHEAD
OF THE POLICE.

PROHIBITION WAS SUPPOSED TO CUT
THE CRIME RATE. INSTEAD, IT MADE
ORGANIZED CRIME MORE POWERFUL. THE
EXPERIMENT ENDED IN 1933.

Chapter 2
College Days

Like a lot of boys, Dutch wanted to be a sports star. He was always a good swimmer, but he had never done well at team sports. He couldn't seem to catch balls or aim well when he threw. One day, Dutch happened to try on his mother's eyeglasses. Suddenly, he could see! All his life he had been nearsighted but didn't realize it. He had just assumed that the world looked fuzzy to everyone.

Nelle took Dutch to an eye doctor. He came away with thick, horn-rimmed glasses. The kids at school teased him a little. He didn't care. He wore his glasses to play sports and did much better.

Baseball was his favorite sport, but he never became a really good hitter. At the plate, he was "ball-shy." Maybe he still couldn't see the ball as

well as the other boys did. But
Dutch ran track, and he also made
his high-school football team.

By this time, the Reagans
had settled down in Dixon,
Illinois. Dutch felt at home
in Dixon. After years of
being a loner, he was one
of the most popular boys
in his class at Northside
High School.

Besides playing football, he starred in school plays and worked on the yearbook. He wrote short stories for the literary contest and took art classes. He was elected president of the drama club and president of his senior class.

When he graduated in 1928, each student was asked to pick a quotation that would be printed under his or her picture in the yearbook. Dutch chose one from a poem his mother had taught him: "Life is just one grand, sweet song: so start the music."

Mugs and Dutch

Dutch's high-school girlfriend was named Margaret Cleaver. She co-starred with him in a drama club production. Margaret was a pretty girl, but for some reason everyone called her "Mugs." Her father was the minister of the church Dutch went to.

Mugs's father was planning to send her to Eureka College. It was a Disciples of Christ school near Peoria, Illinois. When Mugs visited the campus, Dutch went along. He loved what he saw.

Eureka was a small school, but the elm-shaded campus reminded him of descriptions

EUREKA COLLEGE

of Harvard and Yale that he had read about in books.

In 1928 most high-school graduates in the United States went straight to work. Out of every hundred students, only two or three went on to college.

Neil Reagan was already working in a cement plant. Dutch's dad was now a partner in a shoe store in Dixon. He was doing better than before, but there was still not enough money to pay for four years of college.

So Dutch went to see the Eureka College president. He told him that he was an all-around athlete, who would be a credit to the school.

The president was impressed by his confidence. He arranged for a scholarship. Dutch

would earn the rest of his money by working part-time. To help pay for room and board, he washed dishes in his fraternity house.

Almost as soon as Dutch started at Eureka, there was a crisis. The college was short of money and planned to cut out some courses. There was a meeting, and Dutch made a strong speech against the cuts.

Before he knew it, Dutch was leading a student strike. The strike ended with a compromise after a few days. But Dutch was elected to the student senate, becoming president in his senior year.

EUREKA COLLEGE

Reagan — Class of 32

The football coach was another problem. He took one look at Dutch and decided he was too small for football. Dutch was still growing. He trained hard for a year to build himself up. In his sophomore year, he became a varsity guard.

Dutch was just an average student at Eureka. But he was so busy that it was a miracle he passed his courses at all. Besides playing football, he was also the star of the swimming team and the track team.

When basketball season started, he became a cheerleader and president of the Boosters Club. He was a reporter for the school paper and an editor of the yearbook. He starred in seven class plays and won a prize in an acting contest at Northwestern University.

"You could make it as an actor," one judge told him. That sounded exciting but not very practical.

While Dutch was studying at college, the country had fallen on hard times. The stock market crashed in October 1929. The country entered what became known as the Great Depression. Jack Reagan had lost his shoe store. Neil was out of work. The family was getting by on what Nelle earned sewing.

GREAT DEPRESSION

THE GREAT DEPRESSION BEGAN WITH THE STOCK MARKET CRASH ON BLACK THURSDAY, OCTOBER 24, 1929. IN A FEW SHORT DAYS, MANY MILLIONAIRES LOST ALL THEIR MONEY.

THOUSANDS OF BANKS AND BUSINESSES SOON CLOSED. MILLIONS FOUND THEMSELVES OUT OF WORK. MEN AND WOMEN STOOD IN LONG LINES, WAITING FOR HANDOUTS OF BREAD AND SOUP.

MANY FARMERS LOST THEIR LAND. WHOLE FAMILIES PILED INTO BROKEN-DOWN

CARS, HEADING WEST IN SEARCH OF PAYING WORK.

FRANKLIN DELANO ROOSEVELT BECAME PRESIDENT IN 1933. HE STARTED GOVERNMENT PROGRAMS TO GIVE WORK TO THE UNEMPLOYED. ROOSEVELT'S POLICIES GAVE MANY PEOPLE HOPE, BUT THE GREAT DEPRESSION DIDN'T END IN AMERICA UNTIL AFTER 1940. EVEN TODAY, EXPERTS ARGUE ABOUT WHY IT LASTED SO LONG—AND WHY IT FINALLY ENDED.

Eleanor and Franklin Roosevelt

Jack was a big fan of the new president, Franklin Delano Roosevelt, who was elected just after Dutch's college graduation. Jack was sure that FDR would lift the country out of the Depression.

Dutch was worried about telling his family that he wanted to go into show business. So he applied for a job at a local department store.

But the store hired someone else. After that, Dutch felt free to look for work in radio. He borrowed Jack's old Oldsmobile and drove from town to town. He would beg the heads of the local radio stations to give him a chance.

Whatever he said must have worked!

Within a few years, Dutch Reagan was one of the most popular sportscasters in the Midwest. He covered college football and Chicago Cubs games for station WHO in Des Moines, Iowa.

Strangely, Dutch didn't get to see the baseball games he broadcast. A reporter at the ballpark forwarded the facts to local radio stations by telegraph. Sitting in the studio, Dutch knew the ball and strike count, who hit the ball and got on base, and who had made an error. He used his imagination to fill in the rest.

One day, in the middle of a game, the telegraph went dead. There was a full count on the man at the plate. Dutch couldn't disappoint his audience, so he stalled, telling them that the batter had hit a foul ball into the stands. Then another foul ball. And another. After nine imaginary foul balls, the situation was getting ridiculous.

Suddenly, the telegraph sprang to life. Dutch was relieved. "Well, he struck out," he told his listeners. Then he hurried to catch up with the action.

In 1937 Reagan was sent to Los Angeles to cover the Chicago Cubs. The team was in spring training there. Dutch got a friend to fix up a screen test for him at one of the big Hollywood movie studios. A week later, he was offered a contract. Dutch Reagan was going to be an actor, after all.

Part of being a movie star was getting a makeover. The studio changed his hair and clothes. It told him to stop wearing his glasses. It even changed his name. "Dutch Reagan" just wasn't a good name for a movie actor. Everyone stood around trying to think of a new name.

"How about Ronald Reagan?" said Dutch.

"Hey, that's not bad," said the man in charge.

That was the end of Dutch Reagan. For the first time in his life, he would be known by his real name.

Chapter 3
Hollywood

Ronald Reagan arrived in Hollywood with a great idea for a movie: It was the story of the famous college football coach Knute Rockne and his star running back, George Gipp. After scoring eighty-three touchdowns for Notre Dame, Gipp died in his senior year—only a few weeks after playing his last game.

In 1940 the Warner Brothers studio decided to make a movie about Coach Rockne. But Ronald Reagan almost didn't get to be in it.

The director thought he didn't look like a football player. Reagan had to bring in pictures from his yearbook to prove that he really had played the game.

In the end, Reagan was cast as young George Gipp. In one of the last scenes, the dying football star is with his coach. He says to use his example to inspire future Notre Dame players. In the movie, he exclaims, "Someday, when things are tough, maybe you can ask the boys to go in there and win one for the Gipper." It

became one of the most famous lines in film history.

Now that he was in the movies, Reagan was able to bring his parents to California and buy them a house. He still found it hard to forgive his dad for getting drunk. But he invited him to come along to Notre Dame for the premiere of *Knute Rockne—All-American*. Jack Reagan was thrilled. A few months later, he died of heart failure. Reagan felt lucky that they had made up their differences.

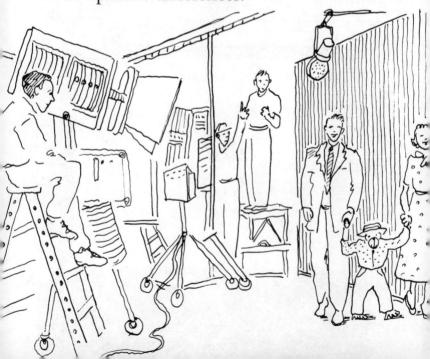

By now, Reagan was starting his own family. On the set of the movie *Brother Rat*, he met a beautiful actress named Jane Wyman. They were married in January 1940.

The fan magazines went crazy over Jane and Ronnie. Stories described them as the ideal movie-star couple. They were

with Jane, Michael and Maureen

glamorous in an all-American way. In 1941 the Reagans had a daughter, Maureen. Four years later, they adopted a son, Michael.

In two years, Reagan made more than a dozen movies. The studio didn't like him to be seen wearing glasses. Movie stars weren't supposed to be nearsighted! So he memorized his parts at home before the shooting started. Luckily, this was easy for him.

Mostly, he played good guys. And he got a lot of attention for being handsome. Art students at the University of Southern California voted Ronnie Reagan their "twentieth century Adonis." That meant that he looked like a Greek god. He thanked them by posing for their art classes.

World War II was raging in Europe, and war movies were very popular. Reagan often played the part of a soldier. In four pictures, he was cast as a Secret Service agent chasing counterfeiters and Nazi spies.

Boys and girls who wrote to the studio were enrolled in a Junior Secret Service Club. They got membership cards signed by the Secret Service "chief," Ronald Reagan. Articles in the club newsletter were written in a secret code that only members could read.

All during his movie career, Reagan enjoyed roles like this. He got to take boxing lessons from an ex-champ named Mushy Callahan. But one day on the set, someone shot off a gun loaded with blanks too close to Reagan's head. He was hard of hearing in his right ear for the rest of his life.

Little by little, he was starting to get more important roles. After playing George Gipp, he was cast in a serious drama called *Kings Row*. In Reagan's big scene, his character wakes up after an operation to find that a scheming doctor has amputated both his legs for no reason. "Where's the rest of me?" he shrieks. That line, too, became famous.

In December 1941 the United States entered World War II. Ronald Reagan was already in the army reserves. His unit made films for the United States Army Air Corps.

U.S. ARMY AIR CORPS

DURING WORLD WAR I, PILOTS FLEW SMALL OPEN-COCKPIT PLANES. MOST AMERICANS THOUGHT OF AIR COMBAT IN TERMS OF DUELS BETWEEN THESE DARING "KNIGHTS OF THE AIR."

BY THE TIME AMERICA ENTERED WORLD WAR II IN DECEMBER 1941, MUCH HAD CHANGED. THE B-17 "FLYING FORTRESS" BOMBER HAD A WINGSPAN OF JUST OVER ONE HUNDRED FEET AND FLEW UP TO THREE HUNDRED MILES PER HOUR.

BESIDES MAKING NEWSREELS SHOWN IN MOVIE THEATERS, REAGAN WORKED ON TRAINING FILMS. THEY TAUGHT BOMBER CREWS HOW TO RECOGNIZE LANDMARKS FROM THE AIR. PART OF THE ARMY'S STUDIO HOUSED A TINY LANDSCAPE THAT LOOKED LIKE ENEMY TERRITORY, SEEN FROM THE AIR. THERE WERE MATCHSTICK BUILDINGS AND FORESTS MADE OF FOAM RUBBER.

Reagan narrated films that told the public about the air corps' latest campaigns. He watched films taken during battles, a lot of them too horrible for the public to see. These images made a deep impression, especially the scenes shot inside Nazi concentration camps. He kept a copy of this reel to show to his children when they were older.

Then the war ended, and Ronald Reagan went back to the movie studio. He made twenty-one more movies. But being an actor wasn't as much fun for him as it used to be.

Politically, it was a difficult time in the United States, especially in Hollywood. In the past, some Americans had belonged to the Communist Party. Now World War II was over and the Soviet Union, a Communist country, was America's number one enemy. In Congress, a committee was investigating Communist activities in Hollywood.

Ronald Reagan was elected president of the actors' union, called the Screen Actors Guild. It was a tough job. Some of his movie star friends warned him that Communists in the United

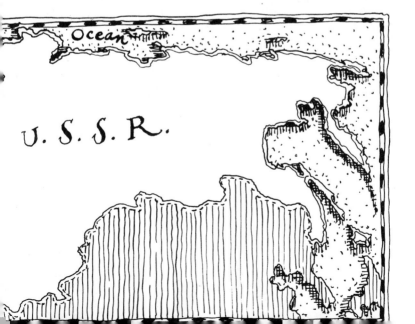

States—people loyal to the Soviet Union—were using the unions to gain power in Hollywood. Reagan was against Communism, but he also wanted to protect peoples' rights. He was against blacklisting, which denied jobs

to actors with Communist Party connections.

Reagan told the congressmen that he didn't think they needed to pass any new laws, such as making it illegal to belong to the Communist Party. It would be better to let "democracy do its work."

"If all of the American people know all of the facts, they will never make a mistake," he said. It was something he believed all his life.

Chapter 4
The New World of Politics

At the end of 1947, Jane Wyman told her husband that she wanted a divorce. For a long time, they had been too busy to spend much time together. Still, Ronald Reagan was taken by surprise. He took his daughter Maureen for a ride in the car and tried to explain to her why the family was breaking up. She didn't understand, and maybe he didn't quite

understand, either. He thought other people got divorced. He never imagined it would happen to him.

This was the beginning of a bad time. At a charity baseball game, he got tagged out and took an awkward fall. Somehow, his right thigh bone broke into six pieces. He spent months in the hospital. And when he got out, he walked with a cane for a long time.

The injury didn't help his career. In 1951 he made a movie called *Bedtime for Bonzo*. Reagan played a college professor who adopts a chimpanzee. As an experiment, he tries to teach it right from wrong. Reagan got good reviews as the frustrated "dad" of a misbehaving chimp. But the movie didn't lead to more comedy roles.

More and more Americans were now watching television. The movie studios were losing money. Theaters were a lot less packed

than they used to be. Some people predicted that the movies would die out altogether. Why would anyone pay to go to a movie theater when TV was free?

Of course, the movies didn't go away. But there were a lot of changes in Hollywood. For one thing, producers were looking for new faces that could lure younger people into theaters. Many of the older stars found themselves out of work.

EARLY TELEVISION

IN 1928 CHARLES JENKINS SOLD A MACHINE CALLED THE RADIOVISOR. OWNERS COULD SEE A BLURRY IMAGE PROJECTED ONTO A MIRROR.

PHILO FARNSWORTH INVENTED THE ANCESTOR OF THE ELECTRONIC TELEVISION TUBE AROUND THE SAME TIME. A BASE-BALL GAME, PRINCETON UNIVERSITY VS. COLUMBIA UNIVERSITY, WAS THE FIRST SPORTS EVENT BROADCAST IN 1939.

ONE OF THE FIRST CHILDREN'S SHOWS, STARRING A MARIONETTE NAMED HOWDY DOODY, WENT ON THE AIR IN 1947.

BY 1949 THERE WERE OVER A MILLION TELEVISION SETS, MOSTLY IN BIG CITIES. FOUR YEARS LATER, HALF OF ALL AMERICAN HOMES HAD TV. THE TOP-RATED SHOW WAS *I LOVE LUCY*.

Although his career wasn't thriving, Reagan suddenly found a chance to be happy again.

A director friend introduced him to a young actress named Nancy Davis. On their first date, they stayed out until three in the morning!

Reagan later said, "Sometimes, I think my life really began when I met Nancy."

After they were married, in 1952, they had a daughter, Patti. A son, Ron, came along six years later. Reagan's lonely days were over. He had a family again. Maureen and Michael were living with their mother, but they came to visit on weekends. The children played in the back-yard pool. Sometimes they went horseback riding.

It took money to support a family. So Reagan started to look for work outside the movies. He became an emcee at the Last Frontier Hotel in Las Vegas, telling jokes and introducing the main act. But he missed California and left after two weeks.

In 1954 Reagan became the host of a television show called the *General Electric Theater*. The show featured a different play every week. Often, movie stars were in leading roles. Besides appearing on television, Reagan was GE's spokesman. He spent months every year traveling around the country by train, giving speeches. General Electric had 139 factories, and he visited them all.

Like his father, Ronald Reagan had always idolized Franklin Delano Roosevelt. FDR became president during the Great Depression. He believed in using the power of government to solve people's problems, to make their lives better. Reagan had thought that was great at the time. But he'd recently started to think that the government had gotten too big. The government in Washington, D.C., kept starting new programs. But, Reagan complained, few of them were ended even after they had served their purpose. Reagan came to believe that, in the long run, government created as many problems as it solved.

Reagan was surprised to find that many of the GE workers agreed with him. They

complained about high taxes and too many government regulations. Little by little, he started to talk about these things in his speeches.

In 1962 Reagan's job as GE's spokesman ended. He hosted another TV show for a while. But mostly he traveled around California giving speeches. One day, a group of Republicans came to his house. Would he run for governor—the highest job in the state?

Reagan was reluctant. For one thing, he was a  Democrat, not a Republican. But little by little, he started to think about getting into politics.

Then in 1962 he joined the Republicans. Two years later, Reagan was asked to appear on national television. He was to speak about the Republican presidential candidate, Barry Goldwater. Reagan talked about how too much government

could threaten individual freedom. Goldwater lost to Lyndon Johnson, but many TV viewers loved Reagan.

In 1966 Reagan agreed to run against Governor Pat Brown. An experienced politician, Brown could hardly imagine that people would vote for a Hollywood actor. "Remember, an actor shot Lincoln," he said.

As it turned out, voters liked the idea of a candidate who was new to politics. They thought he might bring new ideas and change for the better.

Voters in California were worried about high taxes and the rising crime rate.

The Berkeley campus of the University of California was all but shut down by student demonstrations. Reagan remembered his own days as

the leader of a student strike. But he thought it was wrong for a small group to keep students from going to class. He ended many speeches

by saying, "*Ya basta*"—Spanish for "Enough, already."

When the votes were counted, Reagan had won the election. His daughter Patti heard the news and burst into tears. Reagan's new career meant that he would have much less time for his children. At one time or another, all four

children felt that they didn't get enough of their father's love and attention. Patti and Ron took the change harder than Maureen and Michael. Most of their friends were Democrats. They often didn't agree with what their dad was trying to accomplish.

Now that he was actually in office, Reagan had to learn fast. Some people thought that he

was against the poor and minorities. But Reagan just had different ideas about how to help. Soon after taking office, he changed certain civil service rules so that more African Americans could qualify for jobs. He also allowed parent volunteers into school class-rooms. Most of all, he wanted to lower taxes. That way working people could keep more of their own money.

By 1968 the state had saved enough to give some back to the voters. Reagan said, "History is clear. Lower tax rates mean greater freedom. And whenever we lower the tax rates, our entire nation is better off."

In 1980 Reagan became the Republican candidate for president. George Herbert Walker Bush was his choice for vice president. The country had a lot of problems that year. Unemployment was

Campaigning with Gerald Ford and George H.W. Bush

high. Inflation had been high for a long time. That meant that a dollar was worth less year after year. Prices kept rising. It was hard to borrow money to buy a house.

Experts were warning that young people shouldn't expect to live as well as their parents had. Things weren't going well for Americans around the world, either. Fifty-two Americans were being held hostage in Iran.

THE COLD WAR

AFTER WORLD WAR II, THE WORLD WAS DIVIDED INTO TWO CAMPS. BOTH HAD NUCLEAR WEAPONS, BUT THE COLD WAR WAS ALSO A WAR OF IDEAS. THE UNITED STATES AND ITS ALLIES BELIEVED IN CAPITALISM AND FREE ELECTIONS. UNDER CAPITALISM, PEOPLE CAN OWN THEIR OWN HOMES, FARMS, AND BUSINESSES. IN COMMUNIST COUNTRIES LIKE THE SOVIET UNION, THE ECONOMY WAS RUN BY THE GOVERNMENT, AND PROPERTY BELONGED TO THE GOVERNMENT. THE COMMUNIST SYSTEM WAS HOSTILE TO RELIGION, FREEDOM OF SPEECH, AND PRIVATE PROPERTY.

ONE BY ONE, THE COUNTRIES OF EASTERN EUROPE WERE TAKEN OVER BY COMMUNIST GOVERNMENTS. CHINA AND NORTH KOREA SOON FOLLOWED. IN 1956, THE SOVIET PREMIER NIKITA KHRUSHCHEV BOASTED THAT COMMUNISM WOULD TAKE OVER THE ENTIRE WORLD. "WE WILL BURY YOU!" HE WARNED AMERICA.

CUBA BECAME A COMMUNIST COUNTRY AFTER FIDEL CASTRO'S 1959 REVOLUTION. SOUTH VIETNAM FELL IN 1975. BY THE TIME REAGAN BECAME PRESIDENT, THERE WERE COMMUNIST MOVEMENTS IN SEVERAL SOUTH AMERICAN COUNTRIES.

THE COLD WAR ENDED IN 1991, FOLLOWING THE COLLAPSE OF THE SOVIET UNION.

Jimmy Carter ☆☆

President Jimmy Carter had been elected in 1976. He said that the country was suffering from "malaise"—a national bad mood. Ronald Reagan was more optimistic. He said that America's greatest days were still ahead. He even believed that the Cold War would not go on forever. People around the world would choose democracy if they had the chance.

Reagan believed that the tide would turn against Communism. Very few people agreed with him about this. It seemed that Communists were taking over more countries, little by little. Afghanistan and Nicaragua would be the next on the list.

When Election Day arrived, the Republicans carried the day. Ronald Reagan took office on January 20, 1981. His running mate, George H. W. Bush, became vice president.

Chapter 5
A Narrow Escape

Ronald Reagan was the first actor ever elected president. Dozens of his Hollywood friends showed up for his inauguration. Even though Reagan had been governor of California, people in Washington

still weren't sure what to think. Did Ronald Reagan know how to be president? Or was he just an actor, playing the role of president?

President Ronald Reagan and First Lad

ncy Reagan on Inauguration Day. 1981

Ronald Reagan was also the oldest person to become president. Less than a month after taking office, he turned seventy. Would a man in his seventies be strong enough for all the work and responsibility that went with the job?

Patti   Nancy   Ronald   Ron

On March 30, 1981, just nine weeks after taking office, Reagan faced his first big test. That morning, he had made a speech at the Hilton Hotel in Washington, D.C. One of the people with him was Jerry Parr. When he was a boy, Parr had seen Ronald Reagan in *Code of the Secret Service*. The movie had made him want to join the Secret Service. Now he was an agent, guarding the president.

As the president and his aides came out of the hotel, two shots rang out. *Pop! Pop!*

James Brady, the White House press secretary, fell to the ground, shot in the head. Seconds later, there were four more shots. *Pop! Pop! Pop! Pop!*

At the sound of the first shots, Jerry Parr and another agent grabbed Reagan and threw him into the backseat of his waiting limousine. Parr jumped on top of him. Reagan felt a sharp pain. "I think I broke a rib," he said.

Reagan coughed into his handkerchief. The blood was bright red and laced with tiny air bubbles. Parr ordered the driver to head for George Washington University Hospital. At the emergency ward, Reagan got out of the limo and walked to the door. Just inside, he sank to his knees, unable to breathe. The doctors discovered a bullet hole under his left arm. The president was rushed into surgery.

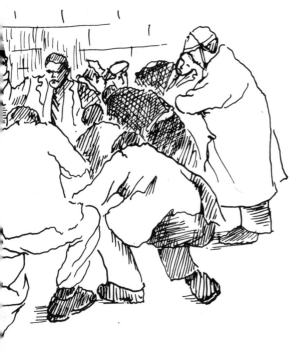

Four people in all were shot that day, including a policeman and a Secret Service agent. James Brady, the most seriously injured, was disabled for life. The assassin was a young man named John Hinckley. He claimed that he did it to get the attention of the actress Jodie Foster. Later on, when John Hinckley went to trial, a jury decided that Hinckley was insane. He was put in a special hospital.

For Reagan, it was a narrow escape. The bullet had lodged an inch from his heart. Still, he came through in good spirits. When he saw his wife Nancy after his operation, the first thing he did was make a joke. "Honey, I forgot to duck," he said.

Fortunately, he was able to make a strong recovery. Reagan had always liked outdoor exercise. He and Nancy had a ranch in the hills north of Los Angeles where he rode horses and

chopped wood. After being shot, Reagan also took up weightlifting. He was seventy years old, but he worked out every day.

After twelve days, Reagan was out of the hospital, and he had to get back to the problems of the economy. In the early 1960s, President John F. Kennedy had cut

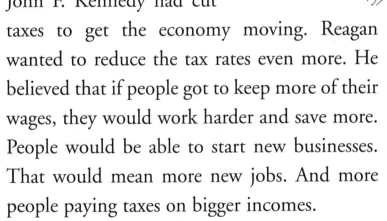

taxes to get the economy moving. Reagan wanted to reduce the tax rates even more. He believed that if people got to keep more of their wages, they would work harder and save more. People would be able to start new businesses. That would mean more new jobs. And more people paying taxes on bigger incomes.

In the meantime, Reagan felt it was important to keep prices and wages from rising.

Congress was still debating the tax cut when nearly 13,000 air traffic controllers went on strike. They were government workers. Their union was asking for a substantial raise. The demand put Reagan on the spot. The controllers' union had supported him when he ran for president. But how could he ask Americans to

put off pay raises if he gave the controllers a big raise? There was also a law against government workers striking. And with no air traffic controllers on the job, the airlines would have to shut down. It was a hard decision, but after Reagan gave the strikers forty-eight hours to return to their jobs, he fired those that did not return. When Reagan announced the firings of the controllers, he said, "I am sorry for this, and I am sorry for them. I certainly take no joy out of this."

Reagan wanted to cut government spending. He wanted a smaller budget. But some programs, like Medicare and free school lunches, were so popular that Reagan gave up asking for any cuts at all. In the end, the budget did not get smaller. It just grew at a slower pace.

One day, a letter came that made Reagan laugh. It was from a seventh-grade student in South Carolina. "My mother has declared my room a disaster area," wrote Andy Smith. Government funds are used in areas hit by disasters such as fire or flooding. So Andy asked for government money to help with the cleanup. Reagan wrote back that "funds are dangerously low." He suggested that Andy make cleaning up his room a volunteer program.

Reagan loved to tell jokes and stories. Like another president, John F. Kennedy, he drew

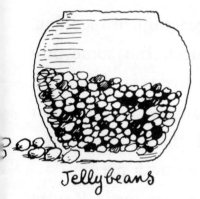

Jellybeans

funny doodles during meetings. He thought most people took themselves too seriously, and he wasn't afraid to look silly. Once, he walked into a cabinet meeting wearing a Bozo the Clown wig!

But even though he seemed relaxed, Reagan got a lot done by keeping to a schedule. A jar of jelly beans, his favorite snack, stood on his desk in the Oval Office. "You can tell a lot about a person's character from the way he eats jelly beans," Reagan often said. Some people grabbed handfuls. Others carefully picked out their favorite colors. When Reagan ate jelly beans, it was usually a sign that his visitor had been talking too long.

It took time, but the economy improved. Meanwhile, Reagan had other crises to deal with. In October 1983 the prime minister of the tiny Caribbean island of Grenada was murdered. There were Cuban soldiers on the island. The leaders of other islands nearby were nervous. Was this part of a Communist plot to take over the whole region?

President Reagan decided to act quickly. Nineteen hundred army rangers and marines made a surprise landing on the island. They fought and defeated the Cuban soldiers. Eight

hundred American medical students who had been trapped in all the confusion were rescued. Later, the Americans found documents that said the Cuban soldiers had been part of a plan to spread Communism through Central America.

The Grenada invasion was popular. Almost two-thirds of all Americans believed that the president had done the right thing. But not everyone agreed. Some thought it was wrong for the United States to interfere in the politics of other nations. Others just worried that trying to fight these battles would cost too many American lives.

Around the same time as the Grenada invasion, 234 U.S. marines in war-torn Lebanon were killed by a terrorist bomb. They were stationed there to try to keep peace. Reagan called this the "saddest day of my presidency, perhaps the saddest day of my life."

"Are we in Lebanon for any reason worth my son's life?" the father of one dead marine asked the president. Reagan told the father that the answer was yes. What happened in the Middle East was "everybody's business," and it was important to fight terrorism.

"Brave men and women have always been willing to give up their lives in the defense of freedom," he explained. But Reagan was faced with a big decision. He would have to send many more troops to Lebanon or remove the ones that were already there. Congress and the people weren't ready to get more involved. So the troops were withdrawn.

It was also part of the president's job to help the country deal with tragedies at home. In January of 1986, the *Challenger* rocket exploded on takeoff. All seven astronauts on board were killed. One was Christa McAuliffe, who had been picked to become the first schoolteacher in space. In schools across the country, children had gathered around TVs to watch the blast-off. They were devastated.

Reagan flew to Florida to speak at the memorial service. In his speech, he spoke directly to schoolchildren who had seen the accident: "I know it's hard to understand, but sometimes painful things like this happen.

It's all part of the process of exploration and discovery. It's all part of taking a chance and expanding man's horizons. The future doesn't belong to the faint-hearted. It belongs to the brave."

Reagan's ability to give graceful speeches on occasions like this led to his being called the "Great Communicator." But Reagan never cared for this nickname. While he enjoyed making speeches, he said there was nothing special about his communication skills. It was just that he spoke about basic values that his audience understood and shared. As he put it, "I just communicate great ideas."

Chapter 6
Steps Toward Peace

The day Ronald Reagan became president, he was given a small plastic card to carry in his pocket. It contained the secret codes that would launch America's nuclear missiles against enemy nations. If word should ever come that nuclear missiles were headed for the United States, the president had only six minutes to decide whether to launch American bombs. The decision, Reagan was told, could mean killing at least 150 million people. This system was called MAD—for Mutual Assured Destruction.

So far, the threat of a devastating nuclear war had stopped either side from starting an attack. But Reagan couldn't help thinking that six minutes wasn't much time to make such an important decision. "The MAD policy was madness," he thought.

Reagan dreamed of a world where no one would have to live in terror of nuclear missiles. He asked the heads of the armed forces to develop a way to defend against incoming missiles. This project was called the Strategic Defense Initiative, or SDI. But SDI would need years of research and billions of dollars.

In speeches, Ronald Reagan made it clear that the United States was prepared to win the Cold War. He did not waste words—he called the Soviet Union the "Evil Empire."

At the time, the Soviets had hundreds of missiles aimed at cities in Europe and the Middle East. When they refused to remove them, America and its allies decided to install their own missiles in Europe, aimed at the Soviet Union.

President Reagan's foreign policy had many critics. Some thought the new missiles made a Soviet attack more likely, not less. There were big demonstrations in Europe and in America, too. European newspapers compared Reagan to a "gun-toting cowboy." Even so, when he ran for re-election in 1984, Ronald Reagan won in a landslide. His opponent, Walter Mondale, carried only his home state of Minnesota and the District of Columbia.

During Reagan's second term, his popularity suffered because of the Iran-contra scandal. The "contras" were a group of Nicaraguan rebels. They were fighting against the pro-Communist government in their country. The U.S. Congress had cut off funds for the contras. Some officials, however, tried to find ways to support them in secret. Some members of Reagan's national security staff made a deal with Iran. Missiles were sold to Iran, although

CONTRA

this was against U.S. policy. Some of the money the Iranians paid to the United States for the missiles went to the contras.

President Reagan eventually fired the people responsible and apologized on television. Even so, he thought Congress was wrong to pass laws that interfered with the president's right to conduct foreign policy.

Mikhail Gorbachev

The Soviet Union, meanwhile, had a new leader. Mikhail Gorbachev knew that the Soviet Union had deep social and economic problems. He wanted to reform the Communist system in order to save it. Reagan liked Gorbachev, but he also bargained hard. He refused to give up his plan to build a defense against nuclear weapons.

In 1987 President Reagan was asked to make a speech in West Berlin. The speech was delivered outdoors in the shadow of the Berlin Wall.

Reagan challenged Gorbachev to give the people of East Germany their freedom. "Mr. Gorbachev, open this gate!" he thundered.

"Mr. Gorbachev, tear down this wall!"

The crowd roared its approval.

Even some of Reagan's speechwriters thought he had gone too far. But Gorbachev continued to work with Reagan. A year later, the United States and the Soviet Union signed a treaty to ban one type of nuclear weapon. It was an important first step. After the treaty was approved by the Senate, the president and Mrs.

Reagan in West Berlin

THE BERLIN WALL

AT THE END OF WORLD WAR II, GERMANY WAS DIVIDED. WEST GERMANY WAS DEMOCRATIC. EAST GERMANY BECAME COMMUNIST. THE LARGEST CITY, BERLIN, WAS IN EAST GERMANY, AND IT TOO WAS DIVIDED. THE WESTERN PART OF THE CITY, SURROUNDED BY EAST GERMANY, WAS OFFICIALLY PART OF WEST GERMANY. BY 1961 MORE THAN TWO AND HALF MILLION EAST GERMANS HAD FLED COMMUNISM BY ESCAPING INTO WEST BERLIN.

ON AUGUST 13, THE EAST GERMAN GOVERNMENT DECIDED TO SEAL OFF THIS ESCAPE ROUTE. OVERNIGHT THEY STARTED TO BUILD A WALL OUT OF CONCRETE AND BARBED WIRE. IT RAN DOWN THE MIDDLE OF STREETS IN BERLIN. IN SOME PLACES, IT RAN RIGHT NEXT TO THE WINDOWS OF PEOPLE'S HOUSES. WHEN THE WALL WAS FINISHED, IT WAS NINETY-SIX MILES LONG. IT CIRCLED ALL THE WAY AROUND WEST BERLIN.

EAST GERMANS STILL TRIED TO FLEE. SOME TRIED TO CLIMB THE WALL WHILE THE BORDER GUARDS WEREN'T LOOKING. SOME TUNNELED UNDER IT. BETWEEN 1961 AND 1989, 171 PEOPLE WERE KILLED ATTEMPTING TO ESCAPE INTO WEST BERLIN.

Reagan visited Moscow. When they went out for a stroll, they were mobbed by friendly crowds.

Before the visit ended, Ronald Reagan spoke to a group of students. He told them that they were living through an exciting time "when the first breath of freedom stirs the air." No one could say what would happen in the future, but he hoped that it would be the first step toward a "new world of reconciliation, friendship, and peace."

Chapter 7
The Farewell Letter

When President Reagan left office in January 1989, no one could be sure if his policies had succeeded. But before the year was out, the Berlin Wall came down. A three-ton section of the wall was sent to Reagan as a gift. It stands today at his presidential library in California.

Mikhail Gorbachev's effort to change Soviet Communism did not succeed. By the end of

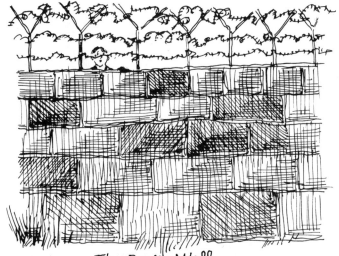

The Berlin Wall

1991, the Soviet Union had broken apart. It was no longer one nation. Ronald Reagan had done his part to help bring the Cold War to a peaceful end. He was firm when he needed to be and flexible when there was hope for change.

The Reagans returned to their home in California. They spent as much time as possible

The Reagans

at their ranch north of Los Angeles. In 1994 Ronald Reagan learned that he had Alzheimer's disease. He was eighty-three at the time. His mother Nelle had died of the same disease, so Reagan knew what was in store for him. Little by little, his memory would fail. In time, he wouldn't even recognize his own children. Even Nancy would become a stranger. He would forget that he had been president.

When he got the bad news, Reagan wrote a farewell letter to the American people. He hoped that by telling people about his disease, he would inspire them to learn  about Alzheimer's and work to find a cure. He thanked the country for letting him serve as president. "When the Lord calls me home, whenever that may be, I will leave with the greatest love for this country of ours, and eternal optimism for its future."

Ronald Reagan lived another ten years, cared for by Nancy. Terrible as his illness was, it helped bring his family together.

When he died in June 2004, Reagan was given a state funeral in Washington, D.C. His casket was carried to the Capitol building on a

horse-drawn caisson—a kind of wagon once used to carry the bodies of soldiers who died in battle. A riderless horse walked nearby, with Reagan's riding boots turned backward in the stirrups. Since the days of ancient Rome, the riderless horse has been a symbol of a departed hero.

A military honor guard carried Reagan's casket up the steps of the Capitol building. People of all ages stood in the hot sun for hours, waiting to pay their respects. In thirty-four hours, more than one hundred thousand people passed by. World leaders came to say farewell. At the end of the viewing, Nancy approached the casket and gently touched the American flag that covered it.

Ronald Wilson Reagan ~ Feb. 6, 1911 ~ June 5, 2004

Afterward, Nancy returned with her husband's body to California. Crowds lined the highways leading to the Reagan library, where he was to be buried. Some people saluted. Others waved tearful good-byes.

Ronald Reagan had lived to be ninety-three, longer than any other president.

Timeline of Ronald Reagan's Life

1911	Born in Tampico, Illinois, on February 6
1928	Enrolls in Eureka College near Peoria, Illinois
1932	Hired as an announcer at an Iowa radio station
1937	Discovered by Warner Brothers Studio
1940	Marries Jane Wyman; stars as George Gipp in *Knute Rockne—All American*
1946	Testifies as a friendly witness before the House Committee on Un-American Activities
1948	Divorced from Jane Wyman
1952	Marries Nancy Davis
1954	Hosts *General Electric Theater*
1960	Delivers more than two hundred speeches in support of Nixon for president
1962	Joins the Republican Party
1964	Makes final film appearance
1965	Autobiography, *Where's the Rest of Me?*, is published
1967	Becomes governor of California
1970	Wins re-election as governor
1981	Becomes fortieth president of the United States; shot outside a Washington Hotel; appoints the first female Supreme Court Justice, Sandra Day O'Connor
1985	Sworn in for a second term at the age of seventy-three
1993	Diagnosed with Alzheimer's disease
2004	Dies at the age of ninety-three

Timeline of the World

Titanic sinks	1912
The United States enters World War I, which ends in 1918	1917
The Charleston becomes popular	1923
The stock market crashes on Black Tuesday	1929
The Wizard of Oz is released in movie theaters	1939
The United States enters World War II	1941
World War II ends	1945
The Korean War begins, lasting for three years	1950
The Supreme Court says segregated schools are unconstitutional	1954
Fidel Castro takes power in Cuba	1959
Civil rights march on Washington, D.C., where Dr. Martin Luther King, Jr. delivers his famous "I Have a Dream" speech	1963
Beatlemania hits the U.S.	1964
Apollo 11 lands on the moon	1969
Woodstock music festival	1969
President Nixon resigns over Watergate scandal	1974
The Vietnam War ends	1975
MTV launches, airing the first music video	1981
The Challenger explodes on takeoff	1986
The Berlin Wall comes down	1989
Gulf War with the U.S. leading thirty-three other nations to drive Iraqi forces out of Kuwait	1991
The Soviet Union collapses	1991
Dolly the sheep is the first successfully cloned mammal	1996
New York's World Trade Center and the Pentagon are attacked	2001
The U.S. goes to war against Iraq	2003

BIBLIOGRAPHY

Cannon, Lou. **President Reagan: The Role of a Lifetime.** Public Affairs, New York, 2000.

Cannon, Lou. **Ronald Reagan: The Presidential Portfolio: A History Illustrated From the Collection of the Ronald Reagan Presidential Library.** Public Affairs, New York, 2001.

Dallek, Matthew W. **The Right Moment: Ronald Reagan's First Victory and the Decisive Turning Point in American Politics.** Free Press, New York, 2000.

D'Souza, Dinesh. **Ronald Reagan: How an Ordinary Man Became an Extraordinary Leader.** Free Press, New York, 1997.

Morris, Edmund. **Dutch: A Memoir of Ronald Reagan.** Random House, New York, 1999.

Noonan, Peggy. **When Character Was King: A Story of Ronald Reagan.** Penguin, New York, 2002.

Reagan, Ronald. **An American Life.** Pocket Books, New York, 1992.

Sullivan, Robert & Editors of Life Magazine. **Ronald Reagan: A Life in Pictures.** LIFE Books, New York, 2004.

Vaughn, Stephen. **Ronald Reagan in Hollywood: Movies and Politics.** Cambridge University Press, New York, 1994.

Weber, Ralph E. & Weber, Ralph A., eds. **Dear Americans: Letters from the Desk of Ronald**

Reagan. Random House, New York, 2003.

Wills, Garry. **Reagan's America: Innocents at Home.** Doubleday, New York, 1987.